THE PROS AND CONS OF DYING

THE PROS AND CONS OF DYING

MAX BIDASHA

To ALL the marvelous people who've helped me on my journey.

Thank you.

I love you.

Contents

A Pro

A pro of dying: everyone is suddenly your best friend

The Most Poetic Thing
You Can Do

I can't write this poem
But you've painted so beautifully
I can't grasp the meaning
There are no absolutes
I feel like a failure
Well, you're still alive
What if I never learn this lesson?
I'm sure there are past lives and more to come
I want to know
Not for my ego, but for
Beauty
Beauty
Fades, but
Poetry lasts forever
Cockroaches live forever
The most poetic thing you can do is
Love yourself
But how can I write that in a poem?

I Feel My Grandmother

When I look in your eyes
I feel my grandmother
I feel my aunties
If I believed in angels,
I'd feel them surround me
Your eyes,
What your eyes have seen
Would break the bones of the weak
What your eyes have seen
Would crush souls
But you would rise up and
Somehow find the beauty in this hell hole
Your hands
Made for hard work
Picking cotton until your
Tiny fingers bled
Somehow you always made time and space for
Love
A deep love
Not always a soft love, but
A deep love

Next Life

In between now and my next life,
Will my spirit get to rest, or will I
Immediately
Become a dung beetle?

My Body

My body is a temple
It didn't fail me

It tired
Like my spirit

My body was wise beyond its years
It fears no human being

Anymore

Where Am I Going?

Where am I going
When I die
'Cuz
I'm really bad at directions

Past Tense

Soon you will speak about me in the
Past tense
It makes sense, but
It still kills my spirit
He was a good man who hated injustice
He had a big heart
He was a cunt who thought
He was better than us all
He'd give you his last penny
He lived wildly
He loved with reckless abandon
He got the hell out of his hometown
He was a whore
He had a good voice, or at least, could carry a tune
He wasn't afraid to die
He lived his life without regrets
I hated him
I envied him
He was alright

Cremation

Cremation: I'll *finally* lose those pesky 200 pounds

Becoming

When I breathe my last breath
I pray I won't be gasping, but
When I do

I'll become memories
I'll become stories
I'll become photographs on your ofrenda

When I'm gone
I'm still becoming

Good Deeds

God,
Please let me die in my sleep
I've done enough good deeds

Simultaneously

Snippets of how things
Used to be
Comfort and console me
And
Depress me
Simultaneously

Respected Wishes

I was once shamed by a deacon
When I said I wanted to be cremated
He said, " we must respect our bodies"
I asked him why we shouldn't respect the
Person's wishes who
Wants to be
Burned and
Turned into
Ashes and
Spread by loved ones at
Their favorite places

Spread me
Sprinkle me

Slowly let the wind take me from your palms
Toss me in the air so high into the ethers where you
won't be able to tell the difference between me and
stardust

Throw me in the bay, but for God's sake
Don't put me in a box to
Rot. I spent my whole life running from them

A Con

If I can miss you when
I'm dead
I will miss you
With the most gut-wrenching longing
My tears will become your rain
I will try to become signs so that
You know I am thinking of you and that
I'm with you
Always
If I could become a ghost
I would haunt your home
Lovingly
It would be my honor to be reduced to
Goosebumps on your arms or
Hummingbirds in your garden
Or a recurring dream
Or a memory that brings tears to your eyes years into
the future
Missing you would, without a doubt, be the single
most difficult
Con
Of
Dying
I can think of

My Heaven

I'm not afraid of
Dying
I'm afraid of the
Unknown
But I know
I don't want to walk on streets of gold
I want to wake up from a dream and hear my
Grandmother's
Pots and pans
And her calling for me to
Come and eat
I want to smell her
Sweet rose perfume
I have to feel her embrace
I need to know she's okay
And she'll tell me she's been waiting for me
Forever and a day
This is my heaven;
Being my Gramacita's mijo again in the same place

Nails and Hair

No, your nails and hair
Do NOT continue to
Grow
After
You
Die

That's an old wives' tale

Stop being dumb

A Pro II

The doctor said
I will die
In
A
Year

I noticed my fair weather friends
Turn to ghosts and
Disappear

This is a pro
To be clear

When I lived longer than my prognosis
The tragedy chasers began to
Furiously look for their next charity case

Another pro
They left me alone

What I found when
I'd surround myself with people who saw past my
Cancer
Was a group of people who loved me
Purposefully
Intentionally
Unconditionally
Fully
And in ways only they knew how

The biggest pro of dying is

Knowing who I am and
Learning the definition of "unconditional"

A Con II

Random fucking strangers
Will, without being prompted,
Tell you their
X, Y, and Z
Died of the same disease,
As if that would ease
The anxiety residing in me

Then I turn around and order my
Fucking coffee
As if some
Random fucking stranger
Didn't just remind me of my own
Mortality

One iced almond milk latte, please

Best Advice

My best friend told me
I can worry until
I die
Or
I can live
It is a choice
He is smarter than he looks

Signs

Anything is a sign
If you look hard enough

Like

Anything is a dildo
If you're brave enough

Can People Cry In Their Sleep?

I don't know why that particular day hit me like a ton of bricks
Grief isn't linear I guess
The moment I opened my eyes they were full of tears
Can people cry in their sleep?
My pillow was soaked
I closed my eyes and went back to sleep
I prayed that I would dream of Gramacita
I didn't

Flush

You used to hold me in
High esteem, now
You hold pieces of me on your mantle.
Your houseguests will walk
Awkwardly around me like
I'm a pet rattlesnake. And
You'll eat take out and
Get drunk, and
Fart in the couch, and I'll be up there
Watching it all go down.
Flush me, already

Stop Crying

Oh, stop crying
Things didn't work out
As I planned, either

-Me From Beyond The Grave

If You See My Bones

If you see my bones

You won't think I don't look:

       Indigenous

Punjabi

                      Mexican

German

You'll be too preoccupied

Staring at my bones

Surreal

There's
Nothing
More
Surreal
Than
Remembering
I'll
Be
Dead
Before
My
Parents

.

Permission To Pass

I held the hand of a man with the
Death rattle
He was fighting like hell to
Keep living
I had to leave the room to shower an old woman, then
Came straight back to room 307
Death filled the
Air
My nostrils
Flared
I touched his heart
Then
His
Head
I told him I loved him and gave him
Permission to pass
I left again to shower another old woman
I ran straight back to 307
He was dead
Was there a slight grin on his face?
Some semblance of peace?
I think there was
I left the room to call hospice, my boss, his family
Then went to wash soiled laundry.
#106 shit the bed

I Am Not Three

Don't say this is a tragedy
I've lived a good life
I'm not an infant who had no chance to
Smell roses
Fall in love
Fly around the world ten times
I've lived a full life
Full enough for three
Don't call this a tragedy
We all must go at some point and
I'm not a three-year-old
Fighting for his life
I've never been homeless or
Abused too badly
This is not a tragedy;
This is life and
Death

Care?

I'm

Dead

What

Do

I

Care?

What Happened?

What happened to your hand,
Shark bite?
Attacked with a
Machete?
What happened to your
Hair?
What is your
Prognosis?
When are you going to
Die?
What do you have?
What happened to/

What happened to
Human decency?

What happened to
Human kindness?

What happened to
Minding your fucking business?

I Lost A Friend To Cancer

I lost a friend to cancer
He didn't have it;
I did
He told me
My cancer was too much for *him* to handle

That
Stung

That
Hurt

It killed me for a while

And yet

I would never wish cancer on him
I know it would be
TOO MUCH FOR HIM TO HANDLE

Disabled

If

  All

    You

      Can

        See

          Is

            Disability

          You

        Are

      The

    Only

  Disabled

    One

Little "c"

It's not cancer
With a big "C"
It's cancer
With a small "c"
It's not God,
For God's sake

I'm Still Here

If hearing is the last thing I'll lose,
I better not hear you crying at my deathbed

You better be telling stories of when
We were young and dumb

You better be reading me
Poetry and
Playing music

I want to hear laughter

I want to hear
Your lips kissing me all over,
BECAUSE

If I can hear,

I'm still here

Palm Springs

My partner is taking
More photos than all the other trips combined
A part of me thinks he's
Just being present and
Enjoying the beauty,
But in the back of my mind
I wonder if he's documenting what could be my last trip to
Palm Springs
Before I die
Either way,
He's got a great eye for photography

Hold Off On Me

Can you just hold off on me
For a while?

Can you just hold off on me
For a while?

And give me one more day to see my mother

And give me one more day to hold my lover

And give me one more day and then another

Death, why don't you hold off on me

And my brother?

Co-written by Marilyn Kaler

I'm Not Sick

I'm not
Sick
I have
Cancer
They expect me to show up to work

Way To Go

What do I want my
Obituary to say?

He died of natural causes?
Too boring

He died of cancer?
Too sad

He died because he was loved so deeply that the love took over
Every cell, tissue, organ, bone until his body couldn't possibly
Contain all the love he had and all the love he was given until he
Exploded from love so strongly that every cell made of love flew
Into the sky and became stars visible to the naked eye

What a perfect
Way to go!

Con III

I won't get to spend my 401k
I can cash it out early and pay a
Huge penalty
401ks are lame anyway

Reasons Why Cremation Makes Sense

I never had kids

After a generation,

Who is gonna give a shit?

I'd just be a headstone that

Birds poop on

Bugs crawl on

Teenagers make out on

Burn me up

Also, cremation is cheaper and

I'm paying out of pocket.

My parents didn't give me money for college so

I'm not holding my breath for this one

All My Exes Live In Texts

My phone is dying

Like me

Sorry if I don't

Return texts

Don't Be Koi

I just overheard

"Koi fish can live up to thirty-five years"

So, if you plan on

Dying in the next three decades,

Don't get a koi fish.

Who will feed it?

Not you.

Hide And Seek

I don't hide
Who I am
To
Seek
Your approval
Not now,
And
Especially
Not
When
I'm
Dead

Dead With A Pulse

Some people are
                    Dead already
Even if they have a pulse
Like when my babysitter and her boyfriend would put scotch tape
On the ceiling so heads wouldn't come out and stare at us
Because they were tweeking so badly
Or when my dad would leave me with a schizophrenic who refused
To take her meds and would scream and fight with the voices in
Her head until her eyes were bloodshot and her mouth was dry
My mouth was dry too because
I was petrified
And terrified
And confused
Or when my grandmother's child-molesting boyfriend would black
Out in our yard while his uncircumcised penis and balls
sunbathed
For all the world to see

I choose to live until it's no longer my choice

Your Doctors

Your doctor told me that if the chemo worked
I'd have a year left to live
But there was a 50/50 chance it would
Your orthopedic surgeon told me that
There was nothing more they could do for my hand
Without even looking at it
Your doctor popped my lung during the biopsy
They said it was common
My lung collapsed
Two of your doctors read the directions on how to properly
Insert a chest tube to inflate my lung
Right in front of me
Right before they inserted a chest tube
To inflate my lung
When I asked if they had done this before
They waved me off and said it was the new model and they just
Wanted to make sure they did it right
Your doctor stood over me and shoved the chest tube between my
Ribs with all of his strength
I told him
I might faint
He told me I was on a bed already
Your doctors treated me like a nuisance
A number
A check
But they sure as fuck didn't treat me with compassion
Your finance department called me
Every single day
Sometimes twice a day
They took their job seriously
I told them what your doctors did to me

(SILENCE)
I told them I had stage IV cancer
I told them I had no left hand and
I told them I had less than a year to be here and that
I lived in my dad's basement
And with my voice cracking, I asked
Do you think they did a good job?
(SILENCE)
Because
You're not getting a penny out of me
And they believed
Every
   Single
      Word
        I
            Said because
They left me alone
To live out the rest of my life

I'd Rather Die

Could you
Imagine if
We *actually*
Died every
Time we'd
Say, I'd
Rather die
Than/
There would
Be a
Lot more
Dead people

Right Hand

I wish I had a

Left hand

Not so I could go
Mountain climbing or
Use a knife or
Tie my shoes
But to steer
So, my right hand could
Be in yours when I
Drive

Your Poems

The saddest part about your
Poems is NOT your poems themselves,
As they are just the

Thoughtful
Beautiful
Articulate
Profound

Retelling of your story
They make me want to
Hold you and tell you
The rest of your life will be the best of your life

Strawberries

My friend
So very full of life
Was dying
Vibrant
Shining
Dying
I brought her
Strawberries
But she refused
Her doctor told her he didn't want her to eat them because
Nobody can wash them
Bacteria sleeps under its seeds
That was such sad news to me
To be deprived of nature's most beautiful thing
She died very soon after
Whether she ate the strawberries or not
And every time I bite into its ripe, red flesh
Your memories dance so lovingly and
Sweetly
Like its juice
How badly I wish we could have eaten
Strawberries together
I miss you...

"fuck cancer"

Two words you will never hear me say
Because
Those two words never helped anyone
Never saved anyone
Never cured anyone
Never brought our loved ones back to life
Never created joy
Never put cancer into remission
But what it did do
For me
Was to
See my world differently
Helped me find my passion
Helped me appreciate the taste of strawberries even more
Helped me learn to write
Helped me know what I am made of
Because of cancer
I met you
I met myself
I learned what true love is, what
True friendship is
Because of cancer
I am here in front of you
Maybe not physically, but what you are
Hearing
Seeing
Holding
Reading is my heart
And spirit
And my wisdom
Because of cancer

I wrote this book
I wrote my plays
I wrote songs
I produced plays
Acted
Sang in front of strangers
Cried
Laughed
Bared my soul
In front of strangers
Lived my life as authentically as possible

Because of cancer,

My dreams are completely fulfilled
I am fulfilled
I am filled to the top with
The kindness you've given me
Love you've shown me
Grace I didn't deserve
Beauty I've witnessed
Sweetness I'm engulfed in

No,
You'll never hear me say "fuck cancer"

Leaving

Are you leaving?
I am
Thank you
I know you were thanking me for my table,
But that triggered the reality of my cancer
Of my mortality
Of my insecurity
You goddamn stranger,
I hope you have the most beautiful day
Ever

Why Did You Fall In Love With Me? I Told You I Had Cancer

There are EIGHT BILLION
People in the world
Why did you have to fall in love with me?
I have cancer
I can die any time
So. Can. I.
You said
And then you loved me
Unconditionally
Wholly
Fully
Like no one was looking until
I accepted your love and
Felt worthy of your love until it became
Self-love!

A Friendly Reminder

If you can read this,

You

Are

The

Lucky

One

ABOUT MAX

Max Bidasha is an Indigenous, Mexican, Punjabi, German, Two-Spirit, disabled, poet and playwright. His plays include, STAGES, Missing Red Girls, The Kids Are NOT Alright, and Mission: Totem Pole. He has stage IV cancer and will continue to write until he's gone. He lives in Napa, California with his partner Joe, boyfriend Armando, and puppy, Momo.

Max Bidasha

Printed in the USA
CPSIA information can be obtained
at www.ICGtesting.com
LVHW041109070624
782591LV00005B/405

9 798218 440442